THE SHOOTING OF DAN McGREW

To Joe & Sharon
Best wishes for Christmas '94

Ted Harrison.

THE SHOOTING OF DAN McGREW

BY

Robert W. Service

PAINTINGS BY

Ted Harrison

KIDS CAN PRESS LTD.

TORONTO

To the dear memory of Martha and Charlie

Kids Can Press Ltd. gratefully acknowledges the
assistance of the Canada Council and the Ontario Arts
Council in the production of this book.

Canadian Cataloguing in Publication Data

Service, Robert W., 1874-1958
The Shooting of Dan McGrew

Poem.
ISBN 0-921103-35-2

I. Harrison, Ted, 1926-   . II. Title.

PS8537.E78S48 1988   C811'.52   C88-093245-7
PR9199.2.S45S48 1988

Kids Can Press Ltd.
585½ Bloor St. West
Toronto, Ontario, Canada, M6G 1K5

88 0 9 8 7 6 5 4 3 2

ROBERT SERVICE arrived in Dawson City when the tumultuous Gold Rush had finally exhausted itself. The adventure was over but its memory would linger for generations to come, a fit subject for writers and poets who desired dramatic human material.

"The Shooting of Dan McGrew" is fictional, but it could have been true. The miners of the Gold Rush were half crazed from the alien conditions they encountered in the new life of the North. The stern, unrelenting cold must have sent the weakest to the wall, and home, ever present in memory, took on an aura almost transcending that of paradise itself.

We are only partially introduced to the main actors in this drama. Our imaginations are left to fill in the missing elements. What relationship does the miner have with the flouncy dancehall lady named Lou? Why is Dan McGrew the object of such insane hatred? Was it love, lust, enmity or greed?

The search for gold has often brought out the best and the worst in people. Greed, jealousy and suspicion are thriving offspring of the precious metal, and it all makes a heady mix when a beautiful woman is also involved.

It is a matter of history that no shooting took place in Dawson City during the Gold Rush. The area was too well policed by the gallant members of the North West Mounted Police to allow lawbreaking of any magnitude to occur. In Alaska, however, the story would ring true. This is not to say that the Klondike was a placid place, just that it was law-abiding. In the American West the settlers arrived before the lawmakers, while in Canada the reverse was true.

Nowadays one can still walk the streets of Dawson City and imagine that one has returned to those far-off days, which appear more golden in retrospect as time erases the sufferings of the past. Honky-tonk pianos still tinkle in the Palace Grand and Diamond Tooth Gertie's. Miners, looking as grizzled as any from the past, still throng the bars and find gold in the creeks. The methods of extraction are more sophisticated these days, but gold still draws many people to chance their luck in the creeks.

I was once told that a "sourdough" is a person who has gone sour on the Yukon and doesn't have the dough to get out. So in the last illustration I picture Lou waving her filched gold poke and preparing to leave for some other green pasture. Will it be Seattle or Vancouver? Nobody knows. But one thing is certain—the old adage is still true: "It's an ill wind that blows nobody good."

The riches one gains from reading Robert Service are many. His poems give a vivid portrayal of the wilderness of the North and how it affects individuals. In this case, the result is not comical but it *is* human, and, as always, it provides food for thought.

Ted Harrison
WHITEHORSE, 1988

A BUNCH of the boys were whooping it up
    in the Malamute saloon;
The kid that handles the music-box was hitting
    a jag-time tune;
Back of the bar, in a solo game,
    sat Dangerous Dan McGrew,
And watching his luck was his light-o'-love,
    the lady that's known as Lou.

When out of the night, which was fifty below,
 and into the din and the glare,
There stumbled a miner fresh from the creeks,
 dog-dirty, and loaded for bear.

He looked like a man with a foot in the grave
      and scarcely the strength of a louse,
Yet he tilted a poke of dust on the bar, and he called
      for drinks for the house.
There was none could place the stranger's face,
      though we searched ourselves for a clue;
But we drank his health, and the last to drink
      was Dangerous Dan McGrew.

Then I got to figgering who he was, and wondering
    what he'd do,
And I turned my head—and there watching him
    was the lady that's known as Lou.

There's men that somehow just grip your eyes,
     and hold them hard like a spell;
And such was he, and he looked to me like a man
     who had lived in hell;
With a face most hair, and the dreary stare of a dog
     whose day is done,
As he watered the green stuff in his glass, and the drops
     fell one by one.

His eyes went rubbering round the room,
        and he seemed in a kind of daze,
Till at last that old piano fell in the way
        of his wandering gaze.
The rag-time kid was having a drink;
        there was no one else on the stool,
So the stranger stumbles across the room,
        and flops down there like a fool.
In a buckskin shirt that was glazed with dirt he sat,
        and I saw him sway;
Then he clutched the keys with his talon hands
        —my God! but that man could play.

Were you ever out in the Great Alone,
        when the moon was awful clear,
And the icy mountains hemmed you in with a silence
        you most could *hear*;
With only the howl of a timber wolf, and you
        camped there in the cold,
A half-dead thing in a stark, dead world,
        clean mad for the muck called gold;
While high overhead, green, yellow and red,
        the North Lights swept in bars?—
Then you've a hunch what the music meant
        … hunger and night and the stars.

And hunger not of the belly kind, that's banished
      with bacon and beans,
But the gnawing hunger of lonely men for a home
      and all that it means;
For a fireside far from the cares that are, four walls
      and a roof above;
But oh! so cramful of cosy joy, and crowned
      with a woman's love—
A woman dearer than all the world, and true
      as Heaven is true—
(God! how ghastly she looks through her rouge,
      —the lady that's known as Lou.)

Then on a sudden the music changed, so soft
      that you scarce could hear;
But you felt that your life had been looted clean
      of all that it once held dear;
That someone had stolen the woman you loved;
      that her love was a devil's lie;
That your guts were gone, and the best for you
      was to crawl away and die.
'Twas the crowning cry of a heart's despair,
      and it thrilled you through and through—
"I guess I'll make it a spread misere,"
      said Dangerous Dan McGrew.

The music almost died away ... then it burst
     like a pent-up flood;
And it seemed to say, "Repay, repay," and my eyes
     were blind with blood.
The thought came back of an ancient wrong, and it stung
     like a frozen lash,
And the lust awoke to kill, to kill ... then the music
     stopped with a crash,
And the stranger turned, and his eyes they burned
     in a most peculiar way;
In a buckskin shirt that was glazed with dirt he sat,
     and I saw him sway;
Then his lips went in in a kind of grin, and he spoke,
     and his voice was calm,
And "Boys," says he, "you don't know me,
     and none of you care a damn;
But I want to state, and my words are straight,
     and I'll bet my poke they're true,
That one of you is a hound of hell ... and that one
     is Dan McGrew."

Then I ducked my head, and the lights went out,
    and two guns blazed in the dark,
And a woman screamed, and the lights went up,
    and two men lay stiff and stark.
Pitched on his head, and pumped full of lead,
    was Dangerous Dan McGrew,
While the man from the creeks lay clutched to the breast
    of the lady that's known as Lou.

These are the simple facts of the case, and I guess
      I ought to know.
They say that the stranger was crazed with "hooch,"
      and I'm not denying it's so.
I'm not so wise as the lawyer guys, but strictly
      between us two—
The woman that kissed him and—pinched his poke
      —was the lady that's known as Lou.

Book design and display typography
by Michael Solomon, Toronto

Set in Caslon 540
by Imprint Typesetting, Toronto

Colour separations, printing and binding
by Everbest Printing Co., Ltd., Hong Kong

The paper is 140gsm Gloss Art
manufactured by Hokaido Paper Manufacturers,
Japan